Sew
a Bag

Sew a Bag

A Beginner's Guide
to Hand Sewing

Amy Karol

ABRAMS, NEW YORK

Editor: Meredith A. Clark

Designer: Laura Palese

Production Manager:
Denise LaCongo

Library of Congress Control
Number: 2019936959

ISBN: 978-1-4197-4063-3
eISBN: 978-1-68335-962-3

Copyright © 2020 Abrams

Photography by Carly Diaz

Cover © 2020 Abrams

Printed and bound in China
10 9 8 7 6 5 4 3 2 1

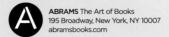

3 How to Sew a Basic Clutch 71

Welcome to the Wonderful World of Sewing!

Sewing a project by hand has so much going for it. Not only is it a perfect way for beginners to get into sewing, it's a skill that all sewers need to learn and will never stop using. And there are many reasons making crafts by hand is so popular. Sewing by hand is:

Meditative. With so many electronics ever-present in our lives, any craft that can be done without electricity becomes magical and comforting—it connects us to the past.

Durable. When done correctly with the right threads and stitches, hand-sewn projects will last for a really long time.

Precise. Using a machine to sew is fast, but it's often hard to get the stitches right where you need them. When you sew by hand, you can make your placement perfect.

Mindful. Our world moves fast, and sewing allows us to focus on just one thing. That said, sewing while listening to music or an audiobook is a wonderful way to do two things at once.

Portable. Sewing machines are heavy and take up space. Hand sewing, on the other hand, takes up almost no room at all. You can take hand-sewing projects anywhere, including on the sofa, in front of the TV, even outside.

Affordable. Sewing machines cost money, which is well worth it if you enjoy sewing bigger projects, but that initial start-up cost can be prohibitive. Sewing projects by hand can cost virtually nothing, especially if you reuse fabrics you already have.

In this book, you'll learn the **basics** for sewing projects by hand, including the tools, stitches, and fabrics used for most **hand-sewn** projects. Then you'll find out how to make a very cute clutch, which may then **inspire** you to explore the wide world of hand sewing.

A **bag or clutch** is a great sewing project if you're just starting out, because you can use fabrics you might already have at home. It's **quick**, **easy**, and uses only a few basic stitches. Almost all the stitching is **hidden**, so if your stitches aren't perfect, it's not a big deal. Also, bags are endlessly **customizable**: you can make them big or small, decorative or minimal. Creating something perfectly tailored to your needs and tastes is the best part of any project!

What Else Can You Sew by Hand?

Once you know the basics of hand sewing, there are lots of projects you can make pretty easily. Bags, hats, mittens, coasters, cozies for teapots and coffee cups, wallets, headbands, scrunchies, book covers, wrist cuffs, stuffed animals, baby bibs—the possibilities are virtually limitless!

For the most part, clothing is sewn by machine, but there is a long and rich history of hand sewing clothes, and it can be done beautifully. Starting with clothes for babies and children is great because they are small. Alabama Chanin in Florence, Alabama, is a clothing company that sells finished hand-sewn garments as well as kits and books on how to sew entire wardrobes by hand. These are wonderful projects to try, because they use simple techniques anyone can master with some patience and time.

TOOLS AND MATERIALS

Sewing by hand requires only a few tools to start. Knowing a bit about different threads and fabrics will also help you select the right materials for your project.

Essential Tools

Here are the tools you'll need for hand sewing just about any basic project including the bag in this book. All can be found at a local craft store or online, and we're willing to bet you probably already own most of these items.

NEEDLES

There are many different types of needles for hand sewing. Which needle you should use depends on the fabric and project. For example, working with leather requires a very different needle from a doll needle, which is used for sewing hair on a doll.

To make your bag, it's a good idea to get an assortment pack of hand-sewing needles (not to be confused with needles for a sewing machine) that has sharps and embroidery needles in a variety of sizes and thicknesses. A "sharp" needle has a rounded eye for thread, while an embroidery needle has a larger, oval eye for floss. While both needles are good for constructing a hand-sewn project, embroidery needles work best for adding decorative stitches.

The needles' sizes will be shown in numbers: the smallest number being the largest and thickest needle, the biggest being the thinnest. So a size 14 is for much finer fabrics, such as silk or a sheer fabric, while a size 8 is for thicker fabrics like cotton or linen.

Always buy the most expensive needles you can; it really makes a difference. Cheap needles will warp and even break, which is frustrating. If you can, buy them at a fabric shop, not at a multipurpose craft store.

EMBROIDERY
SCISSORS

EMBROIDERY
FLOSS

SAFETY PINS

PINS

SEWING
WAX

NEEDLES

THREAD

TAPE MEASURE

THREAD

PIN CUSHIONS

THIMBLE

SNIPS

FABRIC

BOBBINS

PINS

Pins are used to hold pieces together as you sew them. (Mini plastic clamps are getting popular too, but they can only be used on an edge, not anywhere on the fabric, so their use is limited.) Like needles, thinner pins are better for thinner fabrics like silk, and thick pins are needed for thicker fabrics like denim. Straight pins can be used on most anything and are the best way to go if you are on a budget. Ball-head pins are slightly more expensive, but they are also easier to pull out and come in large and small sizes.

THREADS

A good-quality, all-purpose thread made of a cotton-polyester blend is the most versatile thread you can get. Like needles, buy the best you can. Inexpensive threads break and fray and are so hard to work with. Stay away from prepackaged multipacks; they usually have low-quality thread. When choosing thread, try to match the color to the fabric. If in doubt, choose a slightly darker thread color, because that will show less than lighter thread.

Cotton thread or cotton-covered polyester thread is nice to use with natural-fiber fabrics. A silk thread is lovely to use if you are sewing a silk eye mask or a pocket square, but it's a splurge that only you as the maker will experience—the final project will look the same regardless of what thread you use, as long as it's not too thick.

For sewing projects that require a lot of wear and tension on the seams, a heavy-duty thread is a great choice. Find one labeled "upholstery" or "heavy duty." These types of thread, while very strong, are available in limited colors, so they're best used on projects where the seams will be hidden.

SCISSORS

You only need two kinds of scissors to make most projects.

Fabric shears are scissors that are used only for fabrics. Their blades are usually 8 inches (20 cm) long.

Embroidery scissors are smaller, usually 4½ inches (11.5 cm) long, and used to cut and trim threads. These can be plain or highly decorated; have fun choosing a pair that suits you.

Once you've cut out your fabrics and have moved on to the hand sewing part of a project, only the embroidery scissors are needed, which can make your projects very portable. The fabric shears are cumbersome for snipping threads, although they can be used, but embroidery scissors are inexpensive and very handy. For small projects such as bags, you can even use them to cut the fabric. Using your fabric or embroidery scissors to cut paper will dull the edge immediately—even after just one cut—and having them sharpened is inconvenient and costly. Look for both pairs of scissors at a fabric store, and use your office scissors for paper.

Other Tools

Here are a few other basic tools that you don't absolutely need to create your bag or other basic projects, but they do make things easier, especially as you get into more advanced designs.

THIMBLE

A thimble helps you push a needle through fabric, but you really only need one when you're sewing thick fabrics or through lots of layers. Thimbles can be fun to collect at thrift shops and antique stores, but a plain one is easily found at a fabric shop.

PINCUSHION

Pins are often sold loose in boxes, which can easily spill and be a real pain to clean up. That is why pincushions are so popular. They are typically hard-stuffed fabric shapes or magnetic pucks that help you wrangle all your pins and needles.

Magnetic pincushions are usually large and not beautiful to look at, but they are great if you drop all your pins or don't want to push your pins back into a cushion a thousand times. Fabric pincushions come in all shapes and sizes and are, in themselves, a wonderful sewing project to make. You can also buy them at fabric stores in the classic red tomato shape, or in just about any shape imaginable. For portability, a small, stuffed pincushion is easier than a magnetic one.

SEAM RIPPER

These come in handy for taking out little stitches. You can use your embroidery scissors for this purpose, but seam rippers are faster and more precise. You use them by cutting under every few stitches and carefully pulling the fabrics apart. It's tempting to just use it to cut down the middle of the seam in one motion, but it's very easy to slice through the fabric by accident. Best to go the slow-and-steady route.

WAX

Some threads drag and fray, or they tangle when you are hand sewing with them. Using thread wax (sold at fabric stores) to condition the thread first can help keep you stitching smoothly. Simply drag a cut length of thread over the edge of the wax before threading your needle. Thread wax is especially handy when you double your thread—when you thread a single strand through a needle and tie the ends together so you effectively sew with two strands—because it helps the strands stick to each other and act more like a single thread.

ROTARY CUTTER, WEIGHTS, SELF-HEALING MAT, AND CLEAR RULER

Some sewers like to use a rotary cutter for cutting fabric. It's a very sharp wheel that looks like a mini pizza cutter. If you want to use one of these, you'll also need a self-healing cutting mat (so you don't slice up your table) and weights (to hold your pattern down instead of pinning it to the fabric). Cutting against a clear plastic ruler printed with guidelines will help you make a perfectly straight cut. Many quilters use rotary cutters for just that reason. If you are sewing a project that uses mostly straight shapes, these items are useful, but they are completely optional.

IRON

If you are sewing larger items, an iron comes in handy for keeping materials straight as you go. For many small projects this isn't totally necessary, but if you already have an iron and want to give a project a good press, go for it.

Fabrics

Knowing a little bit about fabrics before you start sewing will help you make good choices for your projects. Using the right material for the right project will get you off to a smooth start and will help you avoid frustration.

TYPES OF FABRICS

Fabrics are made out of lots of different materials. They can easily be classified by whether they are made of natural or synthetic fibers. Common natural-fiber fabrics are cotton, silk, linen, bamboo, wool, and rayon (although rayon is manufactured using a chemical process to regenerate cellulose fibers). Synthetic fabrics use fibers that are man-made, like polyester, nylon, spandex, and microfiber. There are also many fabrics that blend the two, like cotton and spandex, or linen and polyester.

Each type of fabric has pros and cons—one might stretch and one might wrinkle. When selecting a fabric for any project, first ask yourself a few questions: Will it have to be washed and/or ironed? Does it need to be strong and durable? Does the fabric's weight work for the project type? (Meaning that if you are sewing a scrunchy, don't choose a heavy-duty stiff denim, or if you're making a potholder, don't use a lightweight, thin fabric.)

A great way to know if a fabric is a good choice for your project is to find a finished version of the project you're making that you really like, either in your closet or at a store, and see what the manufacturer or maker used. You can do this when selecting a fabric for your bag. There is a reason heavy cotton is often used for basic totes!

Entire books are written about fabrics, so obviously there's a lot that you can learn about them, if you're so inclined. You certainly don't have to get into that much detail, though, to pick a smart fabric for your bag or other simple projects. Here's a list of the fabrics you will encounter most often. These are listed by the material they're made from, not by weave. For instance, cotton can be used to make velvet or denim depending on how it's woven.

Cotton

This natural-fiber fabric is very common and used for everything from sheets to garments, and you can use cottons for almost any hand-sewn project. It softens with time and irons very well, but it is prone to wrinkles. It's worth it to look for organic cottons, because growing cotton traditionally uses a lot of toxic chemicals. Reusing cotton fabric is also a great option, especially denim, which is strong and has a nice, natural fading. You'll need to use a thicker needle and thread to hand sew denim, and a thimble will come in handy for protecting your fingertips.

Leather

Leather is a wonderful material to use, but you need thick thread to sew it by hand and an awl, or leather punch, to pre-punch the holes to stitch into. Leather needles are available, and they make the process easier. Leather craft is its own hobby, so if this interests you, finding a leather sewing tutorial online or in a book would be a good place to start.

Linen

This natural fiber made from flax is known for its drape and abundant wrinkles. If you're going for a handmade or rustic look, this is the fabric you want. The weave can be large on this fabric, meaning it can fray easily, so having your seams on the inside is important. It can also stretch and warp, so if you are using it for a tote, you'll want to make it with a strong lining in a heavy-weight cotton.

Polyester and Polyester Blends

If your fabric has some stretch to it, it's likely that it is a polyester blend. Poly blends (such poly-cotton—think of your stretch jeans) have the best characteristics of both fabrics. Polyester itself doesn't wrinkle and is very affordable, but it tends not to breathe, so it retains odor and is difficult to iron. When blended with a natural fiber like cotton, it keeps its stretch, isn't prone to wrinkling, and breathes a bit better. Polyester blends also include nylon, spandex, microfiber, and polar fleece. Some clothing makers stay away from poly and poly blends altogether, but if you are using thrifted fabrics from the '70s, chances are there's a little polyester in there. Dance clothes, hair accessories, and dolls and stuffed animals are all good projects for using polyesters.

Wool

Wool is great for hand sewing, especially if the fabric has been washed and dried several times first. Think of it as controlled shrinking. This creates a dense fabric to work with and helps keep the edges from fraying. Stuffed animals, dolls, and bags are great projects for felted wool. It also makes great patches for a DIY way to mend holes in garments.

CHOOSING FROM THE FABRIC STORE

For small hand-sewing projects, check out fabric remnants that are on sale. They are usually labeled with how big the cut is. Fabric shops often sell cotton "fat quarters" that are typically precut at 18 × 22 inches (46 × 56 cm), which is the perfect size for making small projects. They often come in really fun colors and patterns.

Fabrics that are not precut are sold by the yard. Often stores insist on a ¼-yard (23 cm) minimum for purchase, but sometimes you can buy less than that. Always feel free to ask questions; fabric cutters are there to help you and will tell you everything you need to know about getting the right amount you need for your project.

USING WHAT YOU HAVE ON HAND

It can be so fun and satisfying to go through your castoff clothes to look for fabric for new projects. Drapery, jeans, T-shirts, dress shirts, bedsheets, pillowcases, and sweaters can all be repurposed. Just make sure there is enough of the fabric for the project you have in mind, and that the part you plan to use does not have staining or excessive wear. Sweaters and socks are good for making stuffed toys, T-shirts are good for scrunchies, and tea towels and napkins are good for small bags, wallets, book covers, clutches, aprons, and baby bibs.

THRIFTING FOR FABRICS

There are lots of fabrics in thrift stores, such as bedsheets, table-cloths, curtains, and clothes. A blouse or wool sweater from a thrift store might be enough for several small projects, so keep your eyes open for ways to reuse. Cutting up thrifted clothes can also be an inexpensive way to find silk, leather, and other fabrics that are otherwise quite expensive.

Your Sewing Space

For the project in this book, you don't need a dedicated sewing space, but if sewing becomes a hobby for you, a little more room is helpful—especially if you want to get a sewing machine. Here are a few things to consider.

LIGHTING

Sewing by hand requires good light. Set up near a lamp or use a portable light you can adjust to shine right down on your work. Clip-on reading lights are great for this.

WORKSPACE

For cutting fabrics, a clean kitchen table is fine, just be sure to protect the surface of the table from your scissors. For the stitching itself, you typically don't need a table because you will be holding the project in your hands. Just be aware of posture and tension. Sewing while sitting on a sofa can be great unless you sink into bad posture habits, which can give you aches and pains.

STORAGE

This is personal and can vary depending on how much room you have. A pretty basket of folded fabrics can be put out as inspiration and decoration, or a storage bin that slides under a bed can hold fabrics and clothes waiting to be cut up and will keep out moisture, pests, and dust. Both are great choices. For projects that are not finished, large resealable plastic bags are handy and allow you to be able to spot what's inside them right away. Toss in matching thread along with your scissors, and this makes the project portable and easy to store.

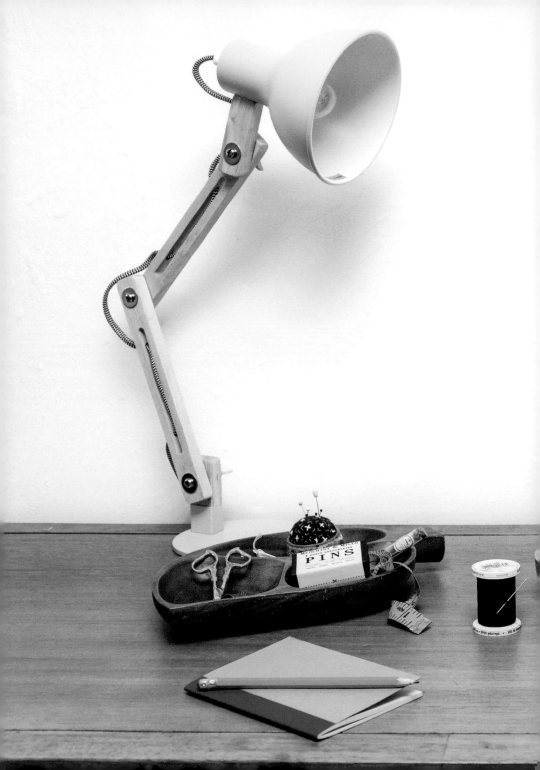

BASIC STITCHES AND KNOTS

Hand sewing has been around for a long time. All items, from clothing to napkins, were stitched by hand until the late 1800s, and they were mostly made with three basic stitches: the running stitch, the backstitch, and the whipstitch. The slip stitch and ladder stitch are also useful to know. When you start out, your stitches may be a little uneven, but the more you sew, the better they'll get. The stitches here are done in a free-form way. Hand sewing differs from machine sewing in its imperfection, and that's often the point. Anything you hand sew will have that handmade quality to it, and that's the whole idea.

BASIC
BACKSTITCH

SLIP STITCH

BASIC RUNNING
STITCH

WHIPSTITCH

LADDER STITCH

Stitch No.1

Basic Running Stitch

This stitch is also known as a gathering stitch, or when made in a longer form, a basting stitch. It's a basic in-and-out type of stitch. It looks like a dashed line on both sides of the fabric. If you pull it tight, it will create gathers. It can be used for adding embellishments but is not typically strong enough for stitching seams together.

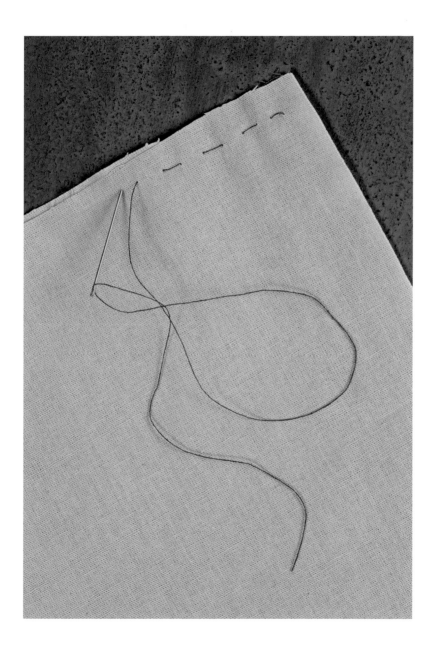

Basic Running Stitch

Stitch No.2

Basic Backstitch

This is the most commonly used stitch when hand sewing seams together, because it is simple and strong. It is like a running stitch but there is a back stitch involved, so that it appears as a solid line on both sides of the fabric. Throughout history, this stitch was used to sew clothing pieces together. The smaller the stitches, the stronger the seam.

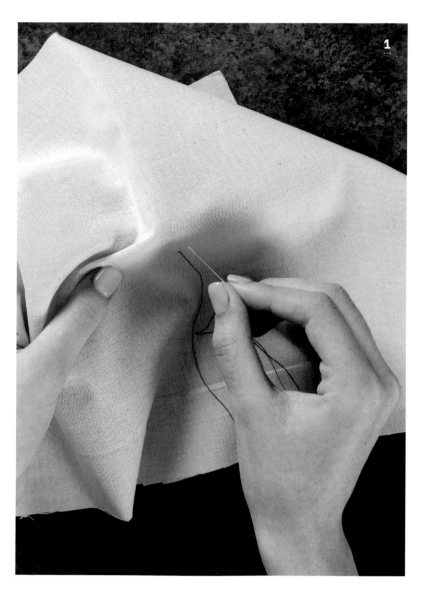

Basic Backstitch

1. Start with a basic running stitch.

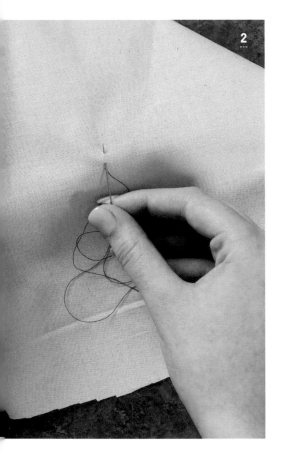

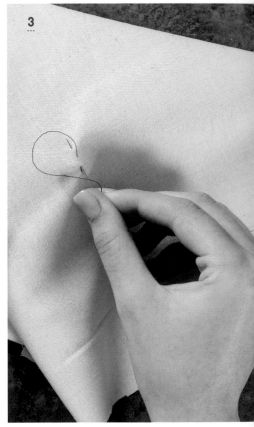

2. Try to make your stitches even in length.

3. After you have a dash of thread on both the top and bottom sides of the fabric, double back and insert your needle at the end of the top layer's stitch. Poke it back out, from the bottom layer to the top, a little ways past your first stitch.

4. Repeat steps 1 and 2 to continue your basic backstitch.

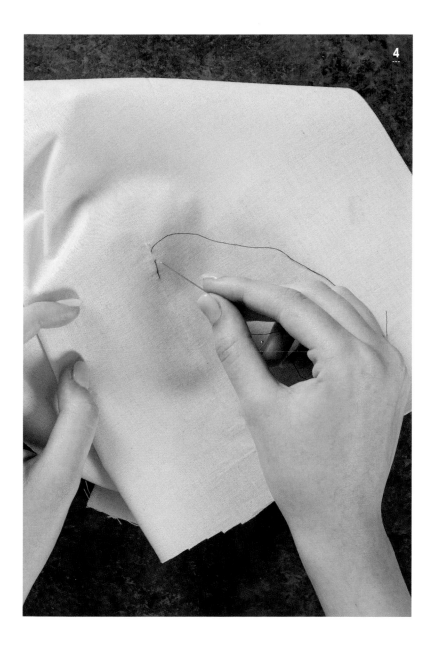

Basic Backstitch

Stitch No.3

- - - - - - - - - - - - - - - - - - - -

Whipstitch

This stitch secures two edges together and can usually be seen because the needle goes up and over the edge of the material to attach all the layers. It can be used as a decorative edge if used with a contrasting thread, and it is popular for making felt toys.

Whipstitch

Whipstitching creates a lovely decoration along the
edge of two layers being sewn together.

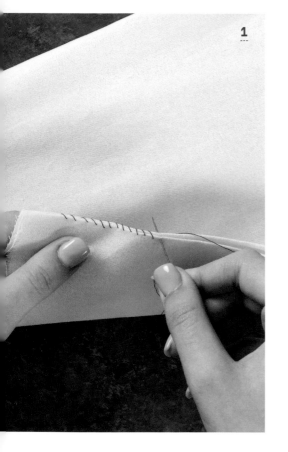

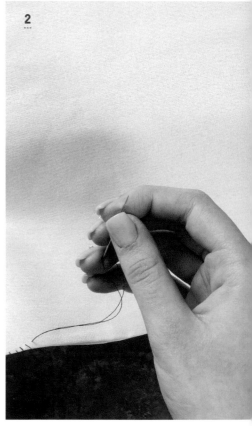

1. Line up your two layers of fabric to create the edge you want, and pierce up through the bottom of the fabric layers to the top.

2. Bring your needle and thread over the edge and pierce again from bottom to top.

3. Repeat along the entire edge.

Whipstitch

Stitch No.4

Slip Stitch

An almost invisible stitch often used for applying appliqués and bindings and sewing hems.

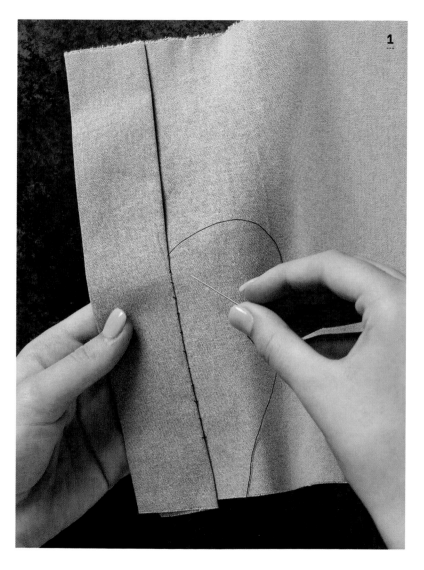

Slip Stitch

1. Fold the edge of the material you are sewing and pull your needle and thread up through the crease of the fold.

2. Prick a tiny amount of the main part of the fabric you're sewing the fold to and draw the thread through.

3. Slip the needle into the fold and back out again. Repeat steps 2 and 3 for slip stitch.

Slip Stitch

Stitch No.5

Ladder Stitch

This is similar to a slip stitch, but it's used when there are two folded edges you want to stitch together, like when you are closing the opening in a pillow or toy after stuffing it.

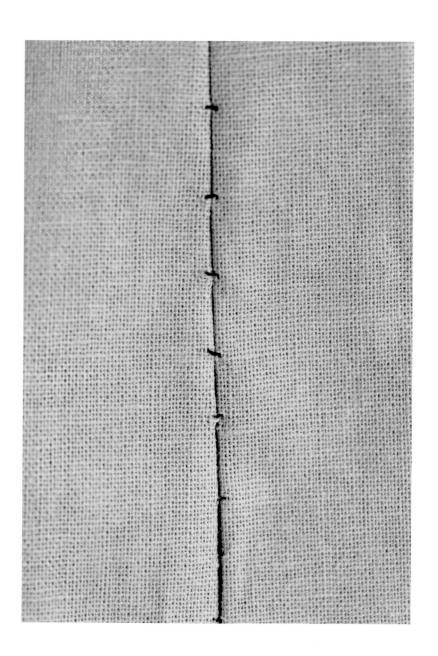

Ladder Stitch

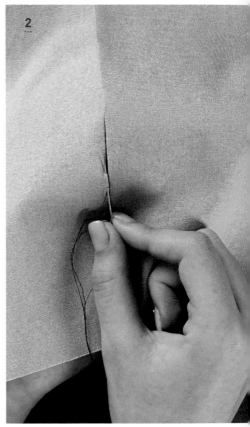

1. Fold both pieces of material and then stitch into the fold on one piece.

2. Go across to the other piece's fold, pierce into the fold and pull the needle and thread along the inside of the fold, and out again.

3. Go back across to the first side and keep repeating. Pull the seam tight to finish, and your seam will be nearly invisible.

Ladder Stitch

How to Start and
How to Stop

Tying Knots

TO START A STITCH WITH A KNOT

To keep your thread from pulling out of your work, you need to start with a knot. There are a few ways to do this. Typically when starting a stitch, you wrap the thread around the needle after it's threaded and pull the needle down through the twisted thread and into fabric to form a knot.

TO END A STITCH WITH A KNOT

To finish your work and make sure your thread won't slip out of the fabric when the seams are pulled on, you need to end with a knot.

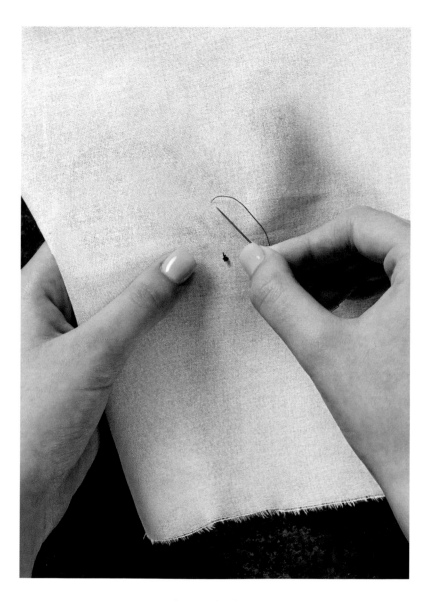

Tying Knots

A starting knot

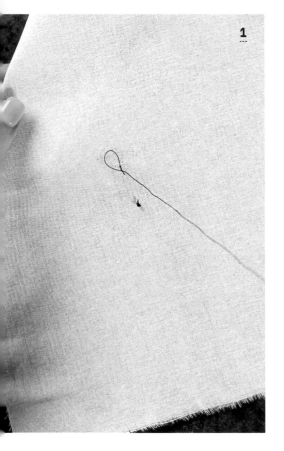
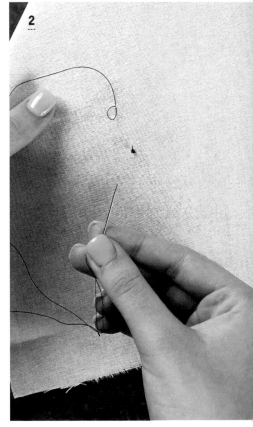

1. Once you've made the last stitch, slip the needle under the stitch before it.

2. This will create a loop with your thread.

3. Pull your thread through twice and do this two more times. Then thread through the fabric and clip close to the fabric.

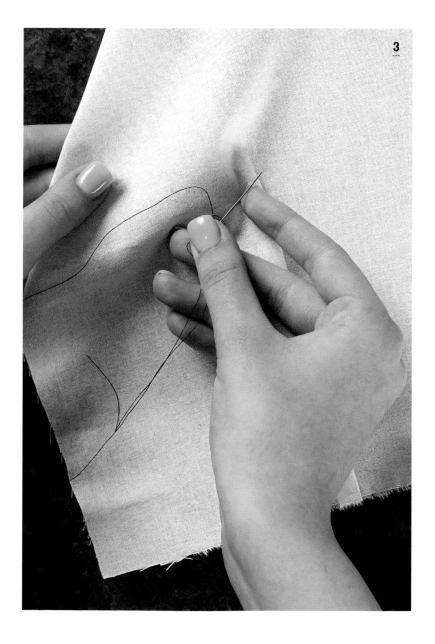

3

Tying Knots

- - - - - - - - - - - - -

HOW TO
SEW A BASIC
CLUTCH

This clutch is very simple to make and can
be created using lots of different fabrics from just about
any material, making it a great project for beginners.
It's basically two bags—the outer fabric is one, and the
lining is the other. It closes by just folding
the top down. I've used black thread on my clutch so
the stitching is easy to see.

It can be minimal and simple in a solid fabric, or ornate and detailed using a decorative fabric. A contrasting bright lining fabric is a fun way to add an additional pop of color. The closure can be as simple as ribbon ties, but you can also use a button and loop, or sew-on snaps. This project can also be made reversible by adding a closure to the inside and outside. This version is folded into thirds when closed, the bottom up and the top folded down and fastened closed. Feel free when making different sizes to just fold the top down and close. It's all very flexible.

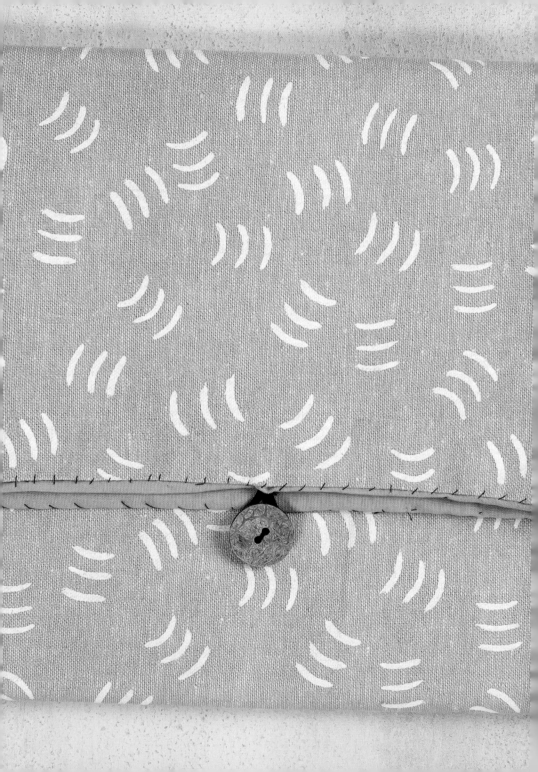

Materials

Outside fabric:
(2) 11½ × 21½-inch (29 × 54.5 cm) pieces of fabric

Lining fabric:
(2) 11½ × 21½-inch (29 × 54.5 cm) pieces of fabric

Paper for making pattern:
(1) 11½ × 21½-inch (29 × 54.5 cm) piece of newspaper, paper bag, or whatever large scrap paper you have on hand

Pins

Sewing needle

Embroidery scissors

Fabric shears

Thread:
all-purpose polyester thread (I like Gütermann Sew-All polyester thread)

Iron

Closure Options

Button and loop:
(1) button and (1) small hair elastic (for the loop)

or

Ribbon ties:
(1) 36-inch (91 cm) piece of ribbon

or

Snap:
(1) sew-on snap size 10 (or larger)

Making Your Pattern

You can make your clutch in any size you like. It can be based on what size feels good in your hand, or how much fabric you happen to have. The measurements given here are for the example bag shown, which when closed is rectangular.

There is a ¼-inch (6 mm) **seam allowance** included, so the finished clutch will be ½ inch (12 mm) smaller overall than the pattern size. If you are making a different size, just remember all four pieces need to be the same size, and you should add ¼ inch (6 mm) to all sides of each piece for a seam allowance.

Making a pattern just means drawing the dimensions of your project using a ruler or tape measurer, then cutting out the measured shape. You can make a **paper pattern** first, or you can just measure the dimensions on the fabric. If you are using the fabric itself as the pattern, lightly mark each dimension with a pencil on just one piece. Cut out your shape and then use that as the pattern to cut the remaining three layers to match.

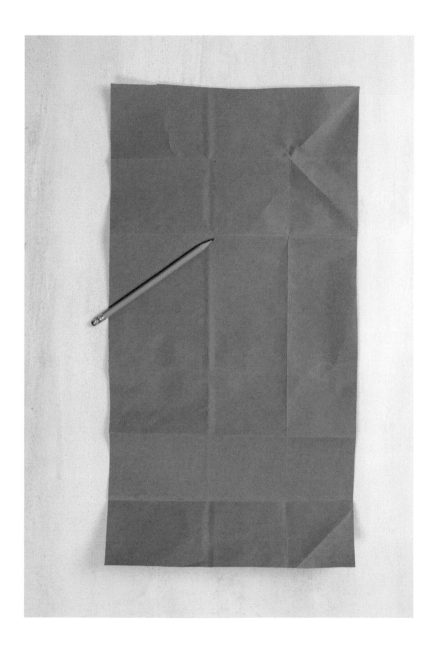

Pinning Your Pattern

With the paper (or fabric) pattern on top, pin it through all the layers of your fabric. To prevent your fabric from shifting, inset a pin at each corner and in the middle. It's better to use more pins than less. Make sure you are happy with the placement of the pattern on the fabric, especially if there is a repeating pattern or a motif you would like to have centered.

Cutting

Cut through all the layers of fabric while they are all pinned together with large, sharp fabric scissors. Press down on the fabric with your hands to keep it in place as you cut.

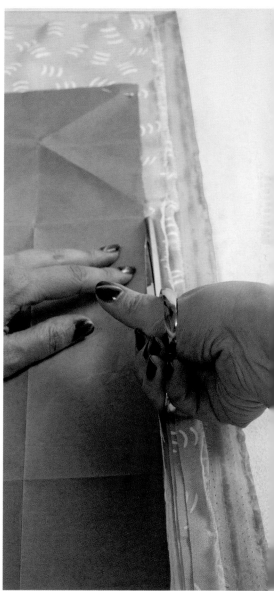

Sewing

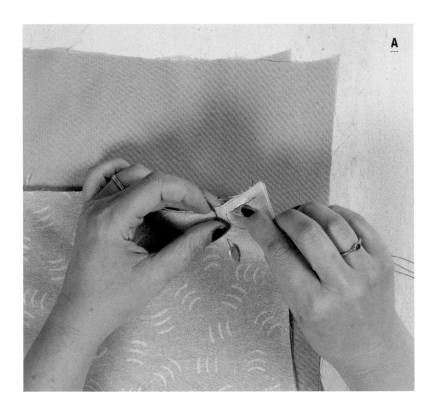

1. Take the two pieces of fabric you want to use for the outside of your clutch and lay one on top of the other, with the **right sides together**. You will be looking at the wrong side of the fabric (the side that will eventually be hidden inside the bag) when you stitch. **A**

2. Starting on one of the long sides, sew a backstitch along that edge as well as the next two edges, leaving one short side open. That will be the top. Stitch ¼ inch (6 mm) from the edge of the fabric and try to stitch in a straight line. Make your stitches as small as possible without losing your mind. **B**

B

Sewing

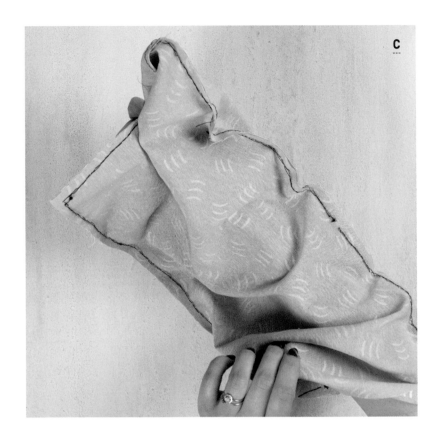

3. Repeat step 1 with the two pieces of **lining** fabric, again with right sides together.

4. Now you have stitched two bags. Turn the outer bag right side out. **C** **D** Iron flat, paying attention to getting the corners pressed out. **Finger pressing** works well here. The lining bag should remain right side in.

Sewing

E

5. Slip the lining fabric bag inside the outside fabric bag; use your fingers to push it into the outer bag for a nice fit. **E** When you peek inside the bag you should see the right side of the lining fabric. The seams should not be visible. **F G**

F

Sewing

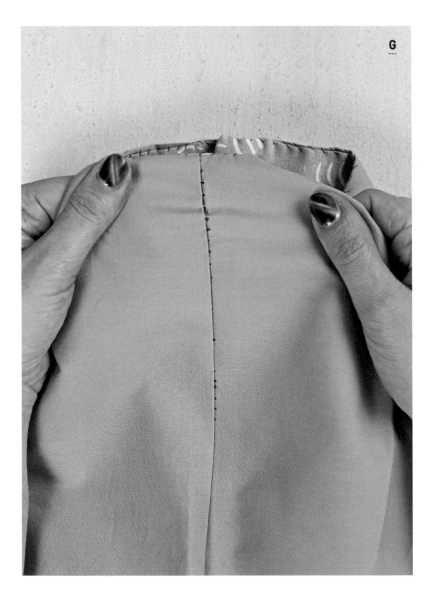

Here is what your lining looks like inside the bottom of the bag.

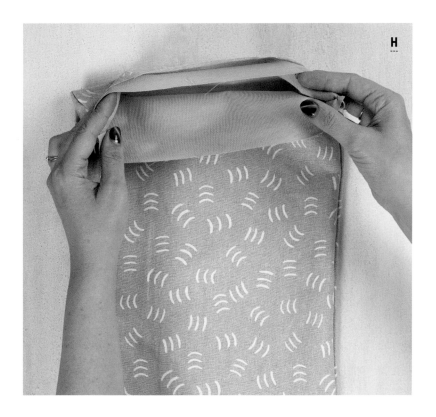

6. Match up the top edges of the lining bag and the outside of the bag at the top opening. **H**

7. Turn ¼ inch (6 mm) of the lining and outer fabrics in toward each other so you have four layers of fabric along the top edge. **I** Iron flat and pin. **J** Using a whipstitch (shown here), slip stitch, running stitch, or back-stitch, sew around the top of the bag opening, starting at a side seam. **K** All these stitches have a different look, and a contrasting thread can be a nice detail. If you want the stitch to disappear, use matching thread and a slip stitch.

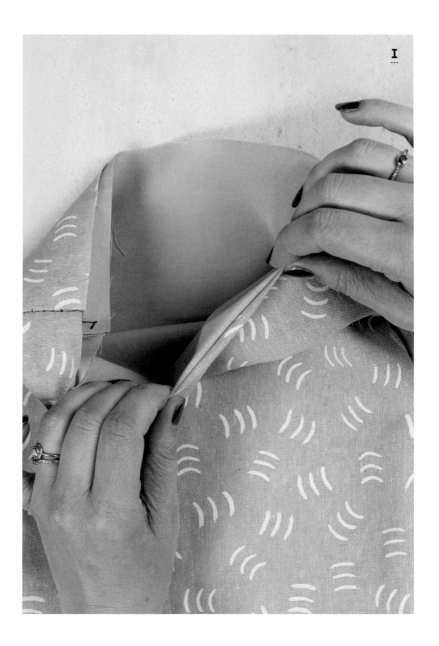

I

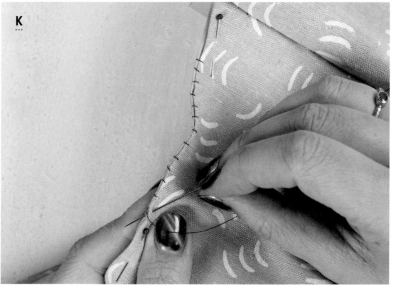

Sewing

93

Adding Your Closure

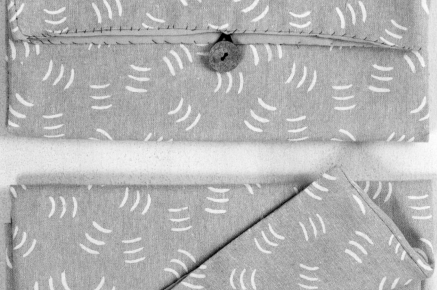

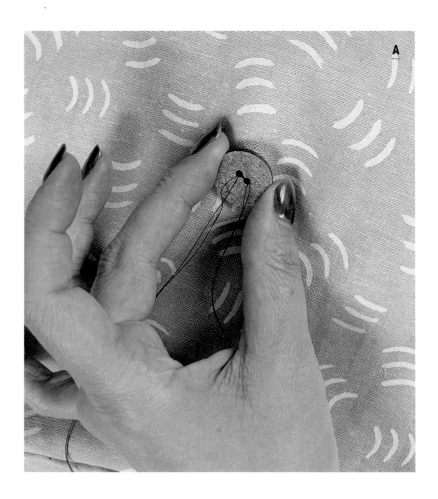

BUTTON AND LOOP

1. Fold the bottom of the bag up one-third. Measure 2½ inches (6.5 cm) from the bottom of the bag, find the center, and mark with a pin. (You may need to adjust the measurement from the bottom to find the center, depending on the size of your bag.)

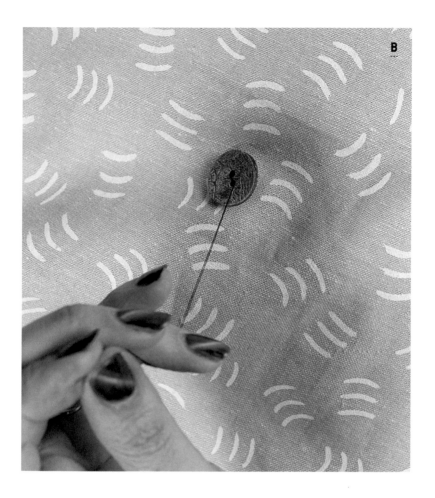

2. Tie a knot using a doubled over strand of thread. Start your stitch inside the bag, pulling your needle and thread through the top layer of lining and top outside layer only, then through the button's holes. Ⓐ Ⓑ Stitch through only these fabric layers while securing all of the button holes two to four times, and then tie off with a knot inside the bag. It's easiest to make this knot with the bag turned inside out.

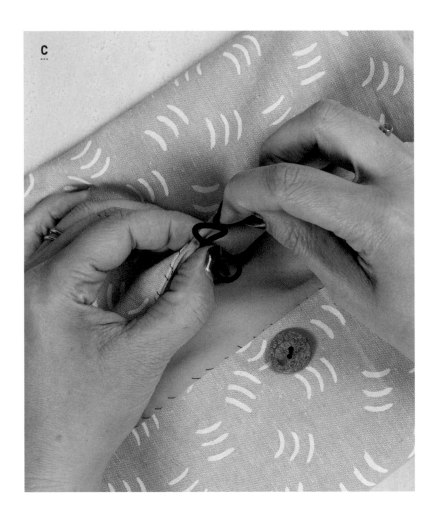

3. Add the loop (the small hair elastic) by folding the top of the bag to just above the button and use that as a guide to mark where the loop should go with a pin. **C** Stitch the loop in place using a whipstitch around the loop, catching only the lining fabric several times, and tie off with a knot on the inside. **D** **E**

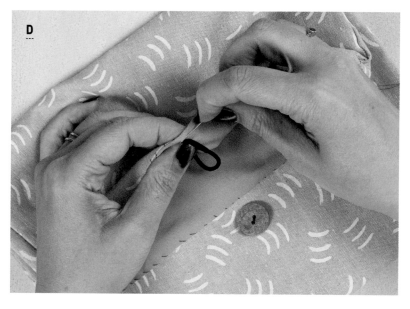

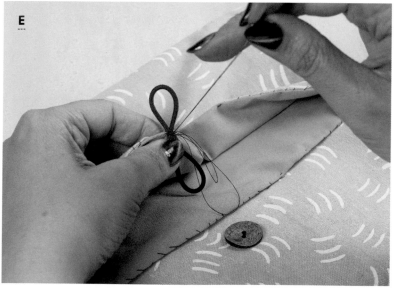

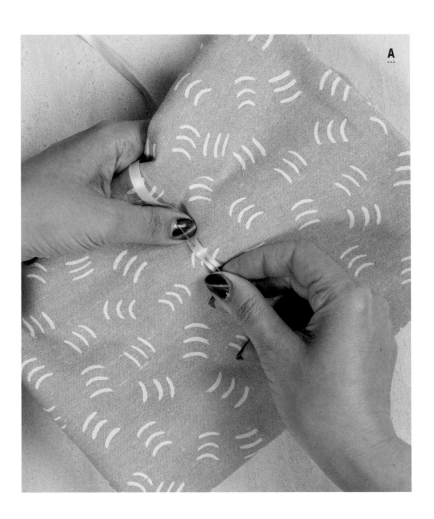

RIBBON TIES

1. Fold the bag into thirds by folding the top down and bottom up to get the desired height when closed.

Adding Your Closure: Ribbon Ties

2. Place the length of ribbon vertically along the back of the bag. Center the ribbon both top to bottom and left to right, and pin it in place. Ⓐ Ⓑ

101

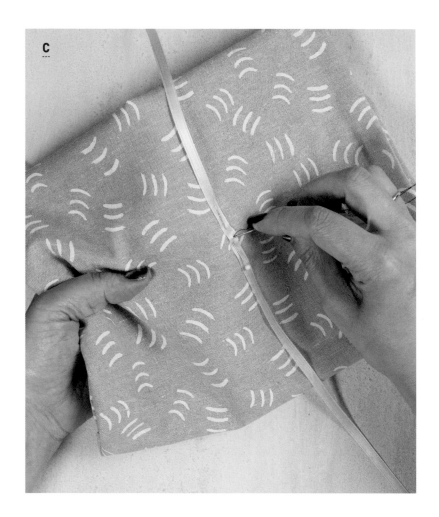

C

3. Sew the ribbon onto the back of the bag at the center point using a backstitch, but only go through to the inside of the bag. (Be careful not to sew all the layers together.) **C** **D**

4. Turn it over and tie a bow, trimming tails if needed. **E**

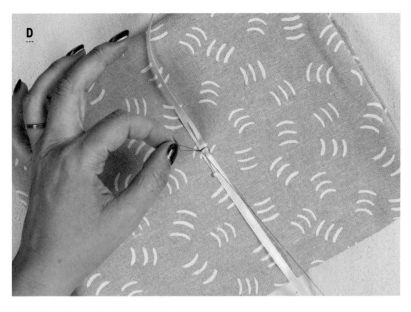

Adding Your Closure: Ribbon Ties

103

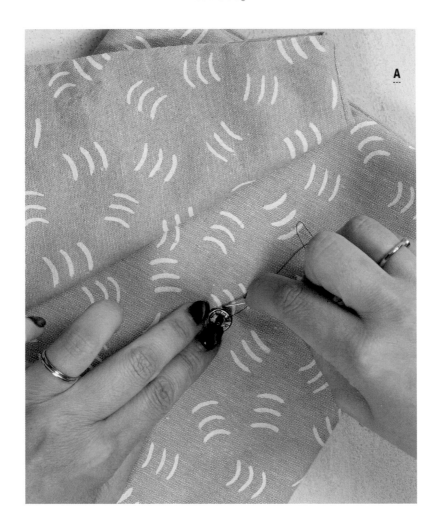

A

SNAP

1. Fold the bag into thirds by folding the top down and bottom up to get the desired height when closed.

2. Mark a spot in the center front for one side of the snap.

3. Stitch one side of the snap in place by making a knot inside the bag and sewing only through one layer of lining and outer fabric. Ⓐ Stitch through each hole of the snap, anchoring it to the fabric two to three times. Ⓑ

4. Tie off with a knot on the inside.

5. Fold up the bag and mark where the other half of the snap should go using a pin.

6. Stitch the other snap side into place, remembering to only stitch through one layer of the outer fabric and lining. Ⓒ

7. Tie off with a knot on the inside.

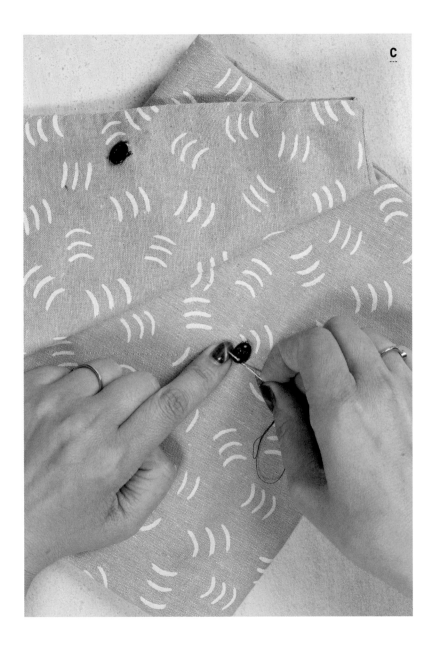

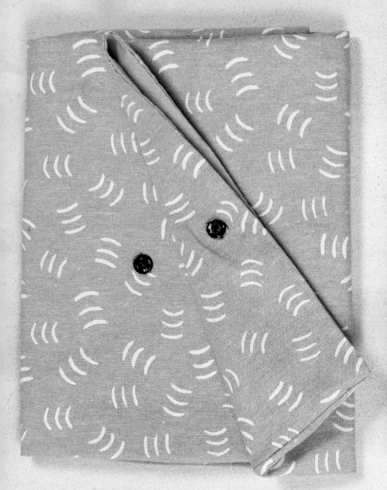

SNAP

BUTTON AND LOOP

RIBBOM

Embellishments

There are many ways to customize your clutch using personalized embellishments such as trim, decorative needlework, and even painting.

ADDING TRIMS AND NEEDLEWORK

Anything you can sew through can be added to make your bag special. Ribbons, silk flowers, patches, beads, sequins—you name it. These embellishments can all be added after your bag is made, just be careful that when you're adding trims or other items, you only stitch through the outer layer and lining layer of fabric so you don't sew your bag shut! Ribbons can be stitched on with a running stitch or backstitch. Patches can be stitched on with a whipstitch. Silk flowers and other items just need a series of stitches and knots to secure as needed.

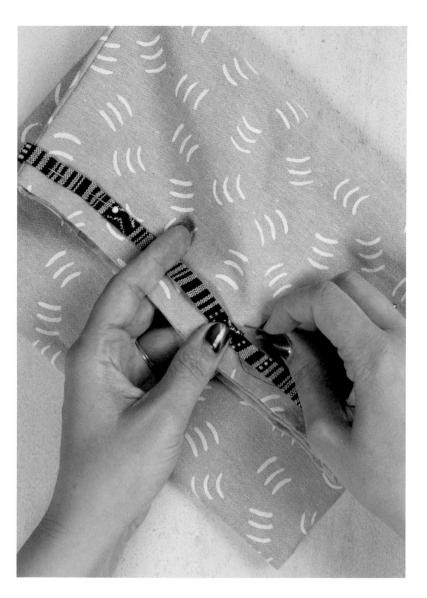

Ribbon trim will make your bag even more special.

Embellishments: Adding Trims and Needlework

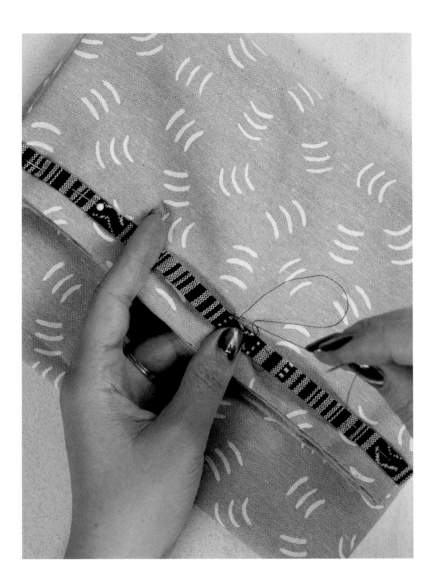

First, pin the ribbon in place.

Embellishments: Adding Trims and Needlework

Then, sew it on using thread in the same color as the ribbon.
Here, a whipstitch is used.

Embellishments: Adding Trims and Needlework

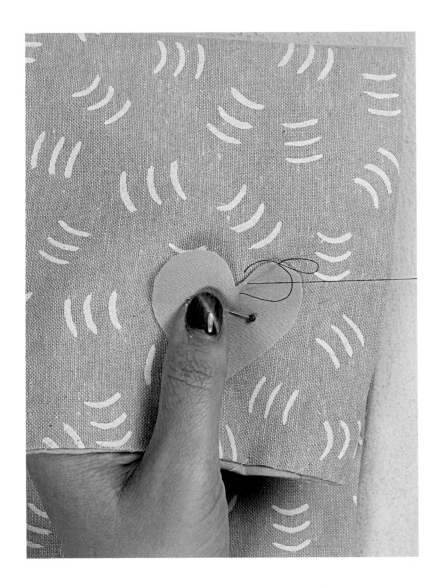

Cut out fabric shapes, like this heart, as embellishments.

Use a whipstitch to attach embellishments.

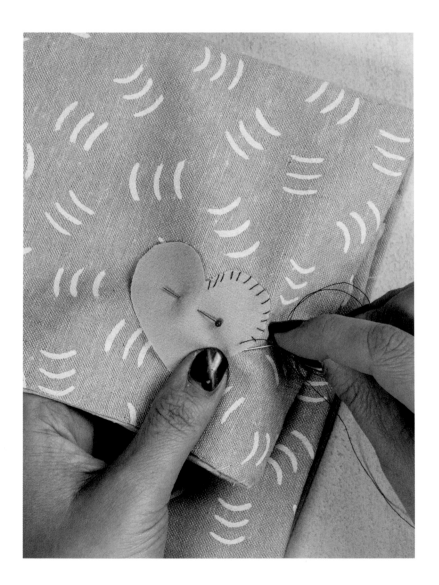

A contrasting color thread will make your
embellishment stand out.

Even if your stitches are a little uneven,
the homespun effect can be charming.

PAINTING ON FABRIC

A plain piece of fabric can be transformed with simple strokes of textile paint or fabric markers. Readily available at craft stores, these paints and markers are specially designed for fabrics, and when heat-set with an iron (always read the manufacturer's instructions) are permanent and waterproof. Simple designs with repeated images are the easiest and create great texture and interest. Think stripes, polka dots, and simple shapes like squares or triangles. Patterns can be applied either before or after the bag is made, but I advise painting your pattern first—if you make a mistake, it's only on a piece of fabric, not a finished bag.

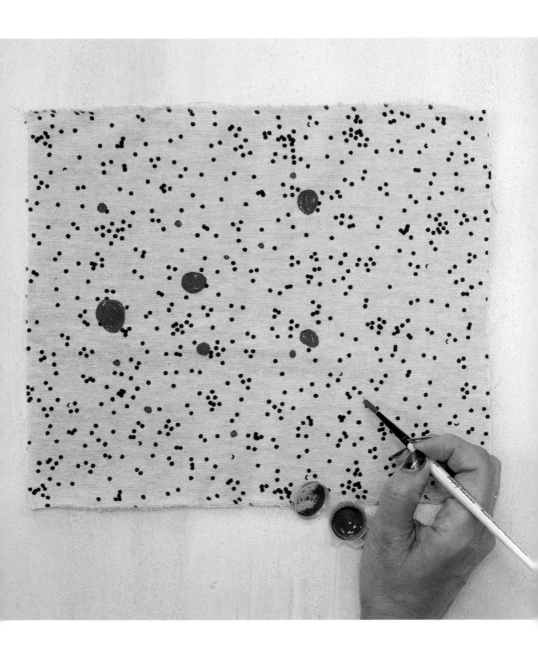

GLOSSARY

As with any craft or hobby, there are some terms that are helpful to know when you're reading instructions or finding out about different techniques. Not all of these are used for the project in this book, but the more you know, the easier it will be to understand and make your future projects.

Appliqué: Applying one piece of fabric on top of another piece of fabric, usually with stitching either by hand or machine.

Basting: Stitching used to hold two pieces of fabric together before sewing with a more stable stitch. This is used when, for whatever reason, pinning won't work or is cumbersome, like when attaching a bodice to a dress or inserting a zipper. It's a large running stitch and is removed later.

Bias: The 45-degree angle that runs diagonally across the lengthwise grain of woven fabric. A piece of fabric "cut on the bias" drapes and can stretch. This is how circle skirts are cut, as is bias trim. Cutting on the bias requires more fabric than cutting with the grain. Bias binding is handy because although it looks straight, it can curve.

Binding: This is an edge treatment used to cover the raw edge of a fabric. It is usually created using bias binding or tape, often in contrasting colors, so it functions as both a finishing technique and a design detail. You can buy premade binding in lots of different colors at the fabric store.

Fabric grain: This is the lengthwise and crosswise thread in a woven fabric. You will hear or read "on the grain," and that means to line up the pattern piece so that it follows the thread up and down, not askew.

Fabric width: The measurement of the fabric from selvage edge to selvage edge is the width.

Finger pressing: Pressing a narrow edge of the fabric down using your finger. This is used a lot on small hand-sewing projects because an iron is often too big.

Hand: This refers to the way a fabric feels and drapes.

Interfacing: A synthetic material, often ironed onto fabric, to give it more strength, support, and stiffening.

Lining: The "inside" of a project, such as the shiny fabric on the inside of a dress or the contrasting fabric on the inside of a bag.

Right sides together: This refers to how to place the fabrics together so after sewing, the seam is hidden on the inside of the project. The right side of a fabric is the side you want to see when you are done. It can also be thought of as the outside. You sew with the right sides facing, then you turn it right side out, or open it flat. Once you do, all you should see is a line, and the stitching and raw edges are on the inside.

Notions: Tool or accessories for sewing—pins, zippers, thread, or anything else used for a project that is not the fabric itself.

Seam allowance: This is the extra space between the edge of the fabric and the stitching line. If a pattern says it has a

¼ inch (6 mm) seam allowance included, you cut out the pattern and sew your seams ¼ inch (6 mm) in from the fabric's edge.

Selvage: The finished edge of fabric that comes off the bolt at a fabric store. The selvage runs parallel to the lengthwise grain of the fabric.

Wrong sides together: The same as right sides together, only the opposite. It doesn't come up that much, but if the front of the fabric is the "right side," the back of that same fabric is the "wrong side."

RESOURCES

FABRIC SHOPS

Bolt Fabric Boutique: shop.boltfabricboutique.com

Modern Domestic: moderndomesticpdx.com

Mood Fabrics: moodfabrics.com

BOOKS

There are a number of great books out there to help you advance in hand sewing and introduce you to machine sewing, as well. Some favorites are:

The Geometry of Hand-Sewing by Natalie Chanin

Sewing Basics by Sandra Bardwell

RECOMMENDATIONS

If you are interested in learning more about sewing and trying other projects, there are a number of great places you can go.

Online sewing communities such as Snippets (getsnippets.com), Textillia (textillia.com), and The Fold Line (thefoldline.com)

Sewing hashtags on Instagram such as #sewing, #sewingtutorial, #sewingprojects

Indie sewing-pattern companies such as Collette Patterns (colettepatterns.com), Noodlehead (noodle-head.com), Sew Liberated (sewliberated.com), and The Fold Line (thefoldline.com/sewing-patterns)

Acknowledgments

Many thanks to all the makers out there who never
want to stop learning, and to the talented team at Abrams
that made this book possible.